FASCINATING FOOD

HOW SUPERMARKETS WORK

BY LIZ SONNEBORN

Essential Library

An Imprint of Abdo Publishing
abdobooks.com

CONTENTS

PIGGLY WIGGLY AND KING KULLEN

Clarence Saunders grew up poor in the American South. As a boy, he worked in the tobacco fields of Virginia. In 1895, at age 14, he found a job more to his liking, working as a clerk in a general store in Tennessee. By the time he was in his twenties, Saunders was employed by a food wholesaler. His job involved traveling to general stores and persuading them to purchase food from his employer.

The type of stores Saunders visited had barely changed during the many decades they had served the American public. Most Americans got their groceries from these dimly lit and barely heated little stores on city streets or on the main roads in small towns. Their wares were displayed out of reach, and a group of male clerks waited on customers from behind a counter. When shoppers

In the first grocery stores, products were on display and customers had to ask clerks to gather the items for purchase.

came into the store, they looked for an available clerk, handed him a list of items, and then waited for the clerk to assemble their order.

The wait could be long. Many of the foods available—such as flour, grain, coffee, and dried fruit—were stored in jars and barrels. The clerk had to measure out the right amount of each item on a scale and bag it. Customers could not handle any of the products themselves; they just had to take what the clerk selected. When the clerk gave the shopper the complete order, he named a price, sometimes basing it on how much he thought this particular customer could pay. The shopper could pay the named price or try to haggle to get a better deal.

For most customers, their food shopping did not end with a trip to a general store. Usually, general stores carried only nonperishable foods, a few items of clothing, and in farming communities, some farm tools and seeds. Shoppers who wanted meat or fish had to go to a butcher or a fishmonger. If they wanted fresh vegetables or fruits, they had to visit a produce store or stand. For baked goods or milk, they had to find a seller specializing in those items. A food shopping expedition could stretch on for hours.

During Saunders's young adulthood, the general store model did see one important innovation. In the late 1800s, factories began to manufacture cheap tin cans and precut, foldable cardstock boxes. For the first time, food manufacturers could put perishable foods in cans. By 1900, packaged foods made up one-fifth of all the products manufactured in the United States.[1] When Saunders worked for the food wholesaler, general stores' shelves were well-stocked with these packaged goods.

THE SELF-SERVICE GROCERY

Saunders offered advice to clerks at the stores he visited, explaining how to shelve items to make them more appealing for the customer. He was bothered by how disorganized most store displays were. But he was even more annoyed at how inefficient the stores were.

Often customers grew frustrated by long waits for an available clerk, and once a shopper got a clerk's attention, it seemed to take forever for him to put the order together.

Saunders became convinced that there was a better way to sell groceries. He was inspired by cafeterias, which had been introduced to the United States at the 1893 World's Fair in Chicago, Illinois. At cafeterias, diners carried a tray and served themselves food from a line of heated pans. Saunders envisioned a similar self-serve model that could make food shopping more efficient and more enjoyable.

On September 11, 1916, Saunders put his theory to the test when he opened the first Piggly Wiggly store in Memphis, Tennessee. A natural showman, Saunders celebrated the event by hiring a brass band and giving out balloons to children and gold coins to their mothers. The customers entered one by one through a turnstile at the store's entrance and were told to take a wooden basket. They then wandered through a maze of aisles stacked with packaged goods. For the first time, shoppers could handle the products themselves and take a good look at their purchases before putting them in their basket.

Unlike at a general store, each item had a price sticker on it, ensuring that everyone would pay the same amount for the same product. At the far side of the store, customers were directed toward checkout lines. After paying, customers left the store by going through another turnstile at the designated exit. The turnstile ensured that shoppers could not grab items and easily run out of the store without paying.

Some of the first shoppers were confused by the small number of clerks. The few Saunders hired were there to stock shelves and operate cash registers. By collecting their own grocery orders, the shoppers themselves were now doing the traditional work of clerks. Because Piggly Wiggly reduced labor costs, it took in higher profits than general stores. Saunders attracted shoppers by passing some of that savings to customers in the form of lower prices.

UNEEDA CRACKERS

In 1890, Robert Gair changed the world of groceries by manufacturing the first easy-to-fold cardboard boxes for packaging food. He pitched his product to the National Biscuit Company, known today as Nabisco, whose leading products included crackers. During the negotiations, Gair's son reminded the company representatives that "you need a name" to put on the box. The boy's words stuck with them. They started selling their packaged crackers under the brand name Uneeda. The new food item became a sensation, and by 1900, the company was selling more than 100 million boxes of Uneeda crackers a year.[2]

The first Piggly Wiggly featured checkout lanes, baskets for shoppers to carry grocery items, and a turnstile before the exit to prevent theft.

Within a few months of opening his first store, Saunders said, "One day Memphis shall be proud of Piggly Wiggly. . . . And it shall be said by all men . . . that the Piggly Wigglies shall multiply and replenish the earth with more and cleaner things to eat."[3] To make that happen, Saunders began to franchise his self-serve store idea to independent grocers. For a fee and a cut of their profits, they could set up their own stores on Saunders's model and use the Piggly Wiggly name. By 1930, there were more than 2,500 of the grocery stores, most of which were clustered in the South and the Midwest.[4]

As Piggly Wiggly grew, other chains adopted Saunders's self-serve model, including Kroger and Safeway. A&P was the largest self-serve chain, with more than 15,000 stores in the United States by the end of the 1920s.[5] At that time, A&P was the largest food retailer in the world.

BIGGER AND BETTER

Like Saunders, Michael Cullen started his grocery career as a clerk. In 1902, he was hired by an A&P store in Newark, New Jersey, and after 17 years with the company, he rose to the rank of division superintendent. He then moved to the Midwest, where he worked for several grocery companies before landing at Kroger. In 1929, he was managing 94 small Kroger stores throughout Illinois.[6]

Also like Saunders, Cullen thought long and hard about how to improve the grocery business. He put his ideas in a

THE PIGGLY WIGGLY NAME

Clarence Saunders was frequently asked how he came to name his grocery chain Piggly Wiggly. He usually tried to avoid answering, although he did once say that shoppers rushing toward clerks in traditional general stores reminded him of piglets eating at a trough, frantically edging each other out to get at the food. Another more likely answer he gave was, "So people will ask that very question."[7] Saunders thought that customers were unlikely to forget his memorable store name, even if it didn't make sense.

letter to William Albers, the head of the Kroger chain. Cullen pitched to his boss a new type of grocery store that he was convinced could revolutionize how Americans shopped for food. He believed the idea could make Kroger a fortune.

Cullen envisioned a "monstrous" store "about forty feet [12 m] wide and hundred and thirty to a hundred and sixty feet [40–49 m] deep."[8] It would be a few blocks away from a downtown shopping area, so the rent would be fairly low, and there would be plenty of room for parking. Not only would his giant store offer customers more variety than ever but it would also have substantially lower prices than any competitor. The huge store would have to purchase so many products that it could negotiate lower prices from food manufacturers.

This high-volume, low-price model would be lucrative enough that the store could afford to sell some products at cost—that is, at the same price the store paid the manufacturer. Cullen's store would feature

By 1918, Piggly Wiggly was opening other locations in Memphis and beyond, or as the aspirational billboard on the side of a location states, "All Over the World."

Tom Cullen, *right*, vice president of King Kullen, offers pastries to a runner from the Soviet Union who was in town for the New York City Marathon.

departments devoted to dairy, meat, and other perishable products, kept fresh through the recent invention of refrigeration. The system would give customers a one-stop shopping experience that would save them time as well as money.

KING OF THE GROCERY INDUSTRY

Cullen was so sure about his grocery store plan that he offered to invest $15,000 of his own money to make it a reality.[9] But Cullen never received a response from Albers.

An employee of the Kroger chain had never passed the letter on to his boss.

Still determined to make his dream come true, Cullen quit his job and moved to Long Island, New York. A few months later, on August 4, 1930, he opened King Kullen in the borough of Queens in New York City. In newspaper ads and flyers, he declared the store the "World's Greatest Price Wrecker."[10] Just as he predicted, the public flooded in.

As word spread about King Kullen, some customers drove as far as 100 miles (160 km) just to take advantage of the store's low prices.[11] This had become an even more important selling point as people struggled to feed their families during the economic downturn known as the Great Depression. Also true to Cullen's predictions, King Kullen rocked the grocery industry. Other chains quickly realized they could not compete with Cullen's stores unless they also adopted his business model.

By 1936, Cullen had 17 stores in New York City and Long Island and planned to expand nationally. But he died suddenly at age 54 following an appendectomy. By that time, Big Bear, Giant Tiger, and other chains of what became known as supermarkets were sprouting up, and approximately 1,200 supermarkets served customers in the United States.[13]

Since then, the supermarket has become an American institution. For most people in the United States, trips to supermarkets are a common feature of everyday life. From their beginnings in the early 1900s, these stores have had to continually adapt to a changing society to attract customers. This has meant adding new products and services or even renovating departments to keep up with trends. As a result, they have become a vital part of American culture. Michael Ruhlman writes in his book *Grocery: The Buying and Selling of Food in America*, "[Supermarkets] are a reflection, even symbol of our culture, and thus a gauge of who we are . . . what we care about, what we fear, what we desire."[14]

CHAPTER TWO

SAVINGS AND VARIETY

In October 1957, 31-year-old Queen Elizabeth II made her first official visit to the United States as the monarch of the United Kingdom. During her six-day trip, she met with President Dwight D. Eisenhower, attended a state dinner at the White House, and toured the National Gallery of Art in Washington, DC. To give her a taste of America's favorite sport, her itinerary included a football game at the University of Maryland.

But Queen Elizabeth was also excited to see a different American institution. After the game, as her royal limousine was heading back to Washington, she asked the driver to make an unplanned stop at a Giant supermarket in a Maryland suburb. For 15 minutes, the queen wandered the aisles in a mink coat as shoppers stared. She was thrilled by the store and the

Queen Elizabeth II's 1957 visit to the United States
included a visit to the Giant Food Shopping Center in
Queenstown, Maryland.

seemingly endless array of goods on display. An assistant manager told a reporter that she had been "quite interested in the frozen chicken pot pies."[1]

Elizabeth II's fascination with a suburban supermarket reflects how the world regarded the United States in the decades following World War II (1939–1945). While other countries were still recovering from the war and the resulting scarcity, the United States seemed like an unbelievable land of plenty. This was demonstrated by the rows and rows of goods available on supermarket shelves. In this way, the supermarket became a symbol of the United States itself, where prosperity and abundance was an everyday reality for many Americans.

In the 1950s, grocery purchases accounted for about 30 percent of household budgets. Today, this figure has fallen to about 10 percent.[2]

THE POSTWAR BOOM

During World War II, as many young American men enlisted in the US Army, small groceries struggled with labor shortages, and some had to close their doors. Supermarkets, however, had staffs that were large enough that they

As supermarkets became more popular, small corner stores and family-owned groceries were unable to compete. Many went out of business.

could afford to lose a few workers without impeding their operations. As a result, supermarkets claimed even more of the food retail market from smaller independent stores during the war. The one-stop shopping experience they provided was also attractive to customers who had to limit store visits because of wartime gasoline rationing.

Following the war, an economic boom in the United States solidified supermarkets as the country's preferred food retailers. In the late 1940s and early 1950s, many American families moved from city centers to suburbs, where many supermarkets were located. Car ownership was also on the rise, making it easier for customers to travel

The grocery cart made it easier for shoppers to stock up on more items and bring small children.

and shop for better prices at well-stocked stores. From 1948 to 1963, major supermarket chains increased their share of the grocery business from about 35 percent to about 50 percent.[3] During this period, small family-run grocery stores largely disappeared.

In the rush to build supermarkets during this period, their boxlike designs were kept fairly simple, with few architectural flourishes. However, most featured modern electrical systems, bright lighting, and equipment to showcase and preserve perishable foods. Essential to nearly all supermarkets was a large parking lot where shoppers could leave their cars for free.

STOCKING UP

Several innovations during this time transformed the supermarket experience. One was the widespread use of large grocery carts. The first self-service groceries gave customers baskets to hold their purchases.

TV DINNERS

Both supermarkets and television came of age in the 1950s and 1960s. Television advertisements were a primary way of marketing new products on grocery shelves. Television also inspired a popular supermarket product of that era—TV dinners. These frozen convenience foods were full meals on an aluminum tray with compartments for entrees, side dishes, and sometimes desserts. After being heated in the oven, they were meant to be eaten while watching television.

But customers became tired when lugging product-filled baskets, and baskets limited the number of goods shoppers could buy on a single trip. To increase sales, grocer Sylvan Goodman of the Humpty Dumpty chain invented the first shopping cart in 1937.

At first, shoppers resisted using carts. Women disliked them because they reminded them of baby carriages, while men feared using a cart made them look too weak to carry their purchases. But carts rose in popularity as more customers carried their groceries home by car, which allowed them to buy a week's worth of food during one supermarket visit.

The weekly shopping trip also became popular because of advances in refrigeration. As more families could afford to buy a refrigerator, perishable foods could stay fresh in their homes for a longer period. The popularization of cellophane wrapping also helped preserve foods. Supermarkets began wrapping meats in cellophane, replacing the paper traditionally used by butchers. Plastic film and wrapping machines also allowed stores to offer packaged fruits and vegetables. New freezer cases were also filled with frozen foods. Clarence Birdseye had developed a method of flash freezing foods in the 1920s, but it was not until the 1950s that advances in freezing technology made frozen foods commercially viable.

COMPETING FOR CUSTOMERS

By the 1960s, the large number of supermarkets operating in the United States meant they had to compete with one another for shoppers. Stores tried to make themselves stand out with exciting and fresh decor. They offered dramatic lighting, colorful murals, and floors covered with patterned tiles or even wall-to-wall carpeting. Displays of merchandise also became more elaborate. Stores featured brightly colored signs with flashy graphics, and soothing music played from overhead speakers.

Supermarkets also competed to see which could offer customers the best amenities. The aim was to make shopping seem less like a chore and more like entertainment. Stations giving out free samples were situated around the stores, and courteous baggers

ICE SHIPPING

In the early 1900s, before the invention of fast freezing, lettuce was preserved during transport through ice shipping. While leaf lettuce was too fragile to ship, a hardy variety called Crisphead could be loaded into cargo cars and covered with a mound of ice. The look of the ice-filled cargo cars gave Crisphead the name it still has today: iceberg lettuce.

offered to carry shoppers' purchases to their cars.

To attract mothers with small children, supermarkets went to great lengths to be family friendly. Many adopted shopping carts with fold-down seats for toddlers. Some built "kiddie corrals," which were areas where children could watch television and play games while their mothers shopped. Some stores had coin-operated rides for children and miniature shopping carts that kids could wheel around, pretending to be grocery customers.

To attract customers looking to keep their grocery bills low, supermarkets began accepting manufacturers' coupons that reduced the cost of prepackaged items. Many also adopted a loyalty program operated by the company Sperry and Hutchinson, which gave shoppers S&H green stamps based on the amount of money they spent.

Customers pasted the green stamps into booklets. They could then use the booklets to purchase items such as small appliances, dishware, and toys from the S&H catalog.

IMPROVING CHECKOUT

One part of supermarket shopping that no one enjoyed was waiting in long checkout lines. Cashiers had to punch the price of each item into a cash register. After paying with cash, customers had to wait for the cashiers to make change. Further slowing down the process, many shoppers paid with personal checks they wrote out while the cashier and customers behind them waited.

In the 1950s, stores tried to reduce checkout times by building round checkout counters and by using conveyor belts to move goods quickly to the cashiers. By 1958, customers started using American Express cards to avoid cash or check transactions. The cards allowed shoppers to pay their bill from an existing account. The nationwide adoption of credit cards in the mid-1960s further eased the checkout process.

In 1974, a pack of gum was scanned at a Marsh supermarket in Troy, Ohio, ushering in possibly the greatest checkout innovation. The new barcode scanner technology

Installing conveyor belts at checkout counters helped reduce the lines and waiting times to pay for groceries.

allowed cashiers to tally up purchases far faster than manually entering them into a cash register. Grocery retailers, wholesalers, and manufacturers worked together to establish the Universal Product Code (UPC), creating a system in which each grocery product had a unique scannable barcode. Scanning not only sped up the checkout line but also gave supermarkets more data than ever on which items sold well and which did not. This helped them better manage their inventory.

THE ADVENT OF THE SUPERSTORE

The 1970s also saw the widespread adoption of another innovation—the superstore, which was much larger than the traditional supermarket. Beginning in 1972, Kroger was particularly aggressive in adopting the superstore model. Most of these stores' additional shelf space was taken up with nonfood items, such as household goods and health and beauty items. During this era, some stores also tried to attract customers by adding a drugstore with a pharmacy to a conventional supermarket.

As enormous supermarkets became the norm, the supermarket industry's leading competitors were small convenience stores. These stores had their origins in a business concept pioneered by John Jefferson Green in 1927. Green was an ice salesman on the docks in Texas. He discovered he could earn greater profits if he also sold food staples such as milk, eggs, and bread. Over decades, his business turned into the convenience store chain 7-Eleven.

From 1959 to 1964, the convenience store model grew quickly as the industry more than doubled its outlets from 2,200 to 4,900.[5] The spread of supermarkets also boosted convenience stores, which attracted customers who did not want to wander through a massive store and wait in long checkout lines just to pick up a few items. Despite their popularity, convenience stores posed little threat to supermarkets, which were still where shoppers made most of their food purchases. In the 1970s and 1980s, however, supermarkets would face new competitors who would challenge their hold on the retail food industry.

CHAPTER THREE

SATISFYING THE SHOPPER

When Joe Coulombe got into the grocery business in the mid-1960s, he was convinced that American consumers were getting bored with the modern supermarket. His view was based on two observations. First, more Americans were going to college, and second, travel by airplane was getting more popular. These observations made Coulombe think that many shoppers were curious people eager to try new experiences. This included new products and new store decor compared with the traditional grocery stores most customers were used to.

When he opened the first Trader Joe's store in Pasadena, California, in 1967, Coulombe stocked the shelves with low-priced products developed by his team to be both tasty and healthy. The store itself looked nothing like a standard supermarket. Inspired by the Jungle Cruise ride at Disneyland,

Trader Joe's aims to make shopping fun, from the colorful murals painted throughout the stores to giving customers floral lei necklaces at grand opening celebrations.

Trader Joe's was decorated with a tiki theme. The checkout stands had thatched roofs, and the employees wore Bermuda shorts and colorful Polynesian shirts. Hawaiian music was piped through the sound system. The decor signaled to customers that shopping at Trader Joe's was fun.

Coulombe was right that at least some grocery shoppers were looking for something out of the ordinary. Trader Joe's became a regional success story before the chain went national starting in the 1990s. Trader Joe's, though, was not the only food retailer to start thinking outside the box. Traditional supermarkets were challenged on several fronts as new food retailers created alternative business models that many supermarket shoppers found appealing.

WAREHOUSE CLUBS

One of the most enduring new types of food retailer was the warehouse club, which was first developed during the economic recession of the 1970s. Founded by Sol Price in 1976, Price Club was the first warehouse club store in the United States. It was located in a converted airplane hangar in San Diego, California. In a no-frills warehouse setting, Price Club offered packaged food that could be purchased in bulk more cheaply than at a supermarket.

Price Club soon spawned imitators. In 1983, Sam Walton, founder of the Walmart discount store chain that sold mostly nonfood items, established Sam's Club. The same year, Jeff Brotman and Jim Sinegal, a former Price Club executive, founded Costco. This warehouse club store featured fresh meat and seafood counters and produce departments to compete more directly with supermarkets. Costco and Price Club eventually merged in 1993.

Sam's Club, Costco, and other warehouse clubs operate similarly. They charge an annual membership fee to customers and offer them products sold at a steep discount. Their warehouses are built in out-of-the-way locations,

GENERIC PRODUCTS

Many supermarkets once had an aisle filled with products in white packaging with their contents indicated only by words such as "potato chips," "corn," or "paper towels" printed in black block letters. Introduced during an economic downturn in the mid-1970s, these generic products reached their peak of popularity in 1983. Generics sold for as much as 50 percent less than comparable brand-name products.[2] But due to their uneven quality, customers abandoned generics, especially after brand-name companies began offering more discounts on their familiar, colorfully packaged goods.

Warehouse clubs such as Costco and Sam's Club are able to offer steeper discounts on items that customers purchase in bulk.

which allows them to save on real estate costs. There are few amenities or elaborate displays, with products often sold directly out of shipping cartons. The stores are able to sell their goods at a low price by keeping costs down and by selling in large volumes. They also offer a limited number of items compared with a supermarket's selection. While an average supermarket sells about 30,000 products, a Costco usually carries only about 4,000.[3]

CHEAP AND CONVENIENT

Supermarkets faced another new rival in 1988 with the opening of Walmart's first Supercenter store. This was a Walmart with a full grocery store inside. During the

1990s, Walmart opened hundreds more across the country, challenging the entire supermarket industry. Undercut by Walmart's low prices, many independent supermarkets and smaller chains could not compete. Failing stores merged with more financially stable chains, causing an era of consolidation. By 1998, just three major supermarket chains dominated the industry—Albertsons, Kroger, and Safeway. Several family-owned regional chains also survived the onslaught of Walmart Supercenters, including Harris Teeter, Publix, and Wegmans.

More competition came from drugstores, many of which began selling milk, eggs, and other staples during the 1990s. Following a period of rapid growth, major drugstore chains such as CVS and Walgreens started stocking a broader array of packaged groceries by the 2010s. They also added grab-and-go coolers with fruit, yogurt, juice, and prepared meals.

ALDI keeps costs low by offering a smaller selection of items, staffing fewer employees, using cart rental, avoiding brand names, and requiring customers to bring their own bags.

After the economic downturn of 2008, dollar stores started to get into the grocery business. These retailers offer discount merchandise, typically priced in whole-dollar amounts. Chains such as Dollar Tree and Family Dollar initially offered packaged foods, but most moved into selling fresh produce, frozen foods, and refrigerated goods. Dollar stores became the fastest growing food retail sector between 2008 and 2020. By 2023, groceries were the top-selling category of goods in dollar stores.

Another option for the cost-conscious consumer is ALDI, the German grocery giant that opened its first American store in 1976 in Iowa. Now ALDI has about 2,000 locations in the United States.[4] The store offers a limited selection of about 1,400 grocery staples in each location, including many from its own label.[5] The simple interior of the stores and low pricing have given ALDI a reputation as a leading discount retailer.

PAYING MORE FOR QUALITY

In the 1970s and 1980s, some grocery customers became concerned about the health effects of foods produced by mainstream methods. For instance, they were hesitant to eat meat from animals injected with hormones and antibiotics or fresh produce coated with pesticides. Advocates of the natural and organic food movement also rejected many products that had been heavily processed by food manufacturers.

Small grocers specializing in natural and organic foods grew to serve these customers. Many such shoppers were willing to pay a higher price for foods they regarded as healthier than the regular supermarket fare. Whole Foods Market, founded in 1980, capitalized on this phenomenon.

The first Whole Foods Market was located in Austin, Texas. It's now the largest natural and organic food grocery chain in the world, with more than 500 locations.

Health-conscious shoppers looking for the freshest possible produce often bypass the supermarket and instead buy their fruits and vegetables at farmers markets. These outdoor markets usually feature several vendors who sell local farm products directly to consumers. Between 1994 and 2019, the number of farmers markets operating in the United States increased from 1,755 to 8,771.[6]

It eventually grew into the first national health food supermarket chain. Whole Foods now competes with several other organic grocery chains, including Sprouts Farmers Market and Fresh Thyme Farmers Market.

Many shoppers are also willing to pay a premium for specialty items or for unusual ingredients. Often inspired by celebrity chefs and televised cooking shows, they are the primary customers for gourmet and specialty groceries. Both in the physical world and online, natural and organic food stores also compete with traditional supermarkets.

Stew Leonard Sr.

"Rule 1: The customer is always right. Rule 2: If the customer is ever wrong, reread Rule 1."[7] That policy helped Stew Leonard Sr. build a family-owned grocery chain that boasts an extremely loyal customer base.

Born in 1929, Leonard inherited his father's milk delivery service in Norwalk, Connecticut, in 1951. By then, most customers had stopped getting milk delivered, preferring instead to buy milk at supermarkets. Leonard decided to establish his own food retailer dubbed Stew Leonard's. At its center was a dairy, where customers could watch fresh milk being bottled. He gradually added new departments, looking to stock the best quality products at the lowest prices he could.

Leonard also wanted to give his store what he called a "wow factor." As customers went down the store's one-way aisles, they encountered singing mechanical characters, including a cow and a celery stalk. The store was also dotted with many free sample stations.

The Stew Leonard's experience delighted new customers as he opened additional stores. He built up such goodwill that serving 44 months of a 52-month prison sentence for tax evasion in the early 1990s barely tarnished his brand. When Leonard died in 2023, Stew Leonard's remained a thriving chain of seven stores in Connecticut, New York, and New Jersey.[8]

FROM FARM TO SHELF

A shopper wanders down a supermarket aisle, looking for something that might appeal to her fussy daughter. Out of the corner of her eye, she spies a colorful cereal box with a cartoon character on it. The shopper quickly scans the nutritional information and determines the cereal is not too sugary. Without another thought, she tosses the box into her cart.

Like most shoppers, she probably has no idea how that box made its way to the supermarket shelf. But it likely arrived there after a long journey, perhaps over hundreds or even thousands of miles. As food products go from being a collection of raw ingredients to an item in a shopping cart, they move through the grocery supply chain.

Breakfast cereals are a go-to meal and snack in the United States. Popular choices are Rice Krispies, Cheerios, Chex, Lucky Charms, Cinnamon Toast Crunch, and Froot Loops.

Cereals such as Kellogg's Corn Flakes are packed into boxes on an assembly line.

THE SUPPLY CHAIN

The cereal box's first stop along the supply chain is the factory of a food manufacturer. The manufacturer buys ingredients for the cereal from a supplier. It then makes the cereal and packages it in the box.

Carefully packed with other boxes of the same product, the box is then transported in a truck to the warehouse of a distributor. The distributor has a contract with the manufacturer to fill orders for the cereal from retail stores selling food. Supermarkets generally do not purchase their products directly from manufacturers, although they might rely on direct store delivery for some specialty or locally made products.

At the distributor, the cereal box is again loaded onto a truck, which takes it to the store. As the truck is unloaded, a store employee inspects the box and scans its barcode to put the product into the store's computerized inventory system. Another employee takes the box to the cereal aisle. If there are old boxes of the same cereal on the shelf, the employee places the new box behind them. This procedure helps move products off the shelf before they reach their expiration dates. After customers buy all the cereal boxes in front of it, the box finally becomes the one facing outward, ready for the shopper to toss it in her cart and take it home for her daughter's breakfast.

THE PRODUCE SECTION

Although it can be a long process involving many companies and workers, a cereal box's movement through the food supply chain is relatively simple because cereal does not spoil quickly. The process is more complicated for perishable goods, such as meat and seafood. Produce is especially fragile, making it difficult to store. Transporting produce is also a challenge because fruits and vegetables must be kept at specific temperatures. They can spoil or become moldy if they become too hot or too cold.

One solution to preserving produce as it travels through the supply chain is to harvest it early so that it ripens in transit. For instance, much of the US supply of tomatoes is grown in southern Florida. They are typically picked when they are still green. The resulting fruit, however, is usually far less tasty than a tomato that has been allowed to ripen on the vine.

Another difficulty is that fruits and vegetables stored together can have an adverse effect on one another. Pears can take on an unpleasant smell if they are stored near garlic. As apples ripen, they release ethylene gas, which can turn bananas brown. When apples are stored in a warehouse, they are often treated with a mix of oxygen and carbon dioxide to prevent the release of ethylene, keeping them in a suspended state. Apples naturally ripen in the fall in the United States. Apples that arrive in a supermarket in August were often harvested about ten months earlier, but they had their natural ripening slowed during the time they sat in a warehouse.

In recent decades, the supermarket industry has adapted the supply chain to satisfy customers' demands for all types

Some truckloads of unripe tomatoes will travel 1,700 miles (2,700 km) from fields in Florida to Terminal Market in Chicago, where they will be distributed to grocery stores and restaurants.

of fruits and vegetables throughout the year. As a result, produce is often grown in distant countries. For instance, Driscoll's, the leading supplier of berries in the United States, is based in California. But when it is not the growing season in that state, the company works with family farms throughout North and South America so that it can provide consumers with berries year-round.

KEEPING INVENTORY

One of the hardest tasks for a supermarket is keeping track of its inventory. Monitoring inventory is a challenge for all stores, but it is particularly complex for supermarkets because, on average, they stock between 30,000 and

40,000 products.[1] The stock of perishable products must be managed particularly closely to remove any foods that are no longer edible.

Computerized systems help supermarkets keep track of inventory. When a product reaches the store or when a customer buys an item, its barcode is scanned. This data also aids stores in determining when to reorder a product. Proper reordering is crucial to a supermarket's profitability. If a store orders too much of the wrong products, they will have trouble selling them and may lose money if the products go bad. But if a store does not order enough of the products shoppers want most, customers will encounter empty shelves and take their business to rival retailers.

Inventory systems also provide chains with information that helps them customize the inventory of individual stores.

REWARDS PROGRAMS

Since the 1980s, supermarkets have used rewards programs to attract loyal customers. By paying an annual fee or simply signing up for free, enrolled shoppers may receive customized coupons or special discounts exclusive to program members. Other common perks include free or low-cost grocery delivery and a gift product on a member's birthday. The programs benefit stores by encouraging customers to keep coming back, and they also provide valuable purchasing data to help chains better understand what their customers want.

Analyzing the data lets them see buying patterns of different neighborhoods. For instance, the shoppers at a store in a retirement community are likely to have different needs from those at a supermarket next to a college campus.

MAKING A PROFIT

Supermarkets often struggle because their business model makes it hard to earn a profit. They have to sell products at a price barely higher than what they paid for them, while their expenses are significant. Michael Ruhlman's book *Grocery: The Buying and Selling of Food in America* outlines the tiny profit margin of Heinen's, a small regional supermarket in the Midwest. Out of every dollar of groceries sold, Heinen receives about 32 cents above what they had paid for those products. Twenty-four cents out of that goes to workers' wages and benefits. From the remaining eight cents, the store must pay rent, utilities, insurance, repairs, marketing, and other miscellaneous expenses, all of which total about 6.75 cents. That means that their profit margin is a meager 1.25 cents on every dollar of products customers buy.[3]

Some supermarket departments are more profitable than others. The grocery department, which includes all the prepacked products in boxes and cans typically found in a store's center aisles, accounts for 27 percent of sales. It includes the profitable and fast-growing sector of wellness products, such as vitamins and supplements. Other high-profit centers include produce, representing 17 percent of sales, and dairy/frozen foods, which make up 15 percent.[4]

A big money loss for most supermarkets is the deli and prepared-foods departments. But since the 1990s, prepared foods have been in high demand by customers, especially parents with full-time jobs and little time to cook for their families. Even though the department attracts many shoppers, the cost of workers needed to prepare sandwiches, pizza, pasta, and other popular dishes is very expensive for stores. If they do not have a prepared food section, they are likely to lose customers to supermarkets that do.

STOCKING THE SHELVES

Essential to operating a supermarket is determining which products to stock. Chains employ different systems for doing this. Some rely heavily on their distributors to select the right products for their stores. Others have teams of employees called buyers assigned to different categories of goods.

Each buyer may make stocking decisions about thousands of products. These decisions are guided less by a product's quality or taste than by how much it contributes to the profit margin. By using sales data, they are likely to avoid stocking low-selling products and popular products that do not contribute enough to the bottom line. Buyers also negotiate with suppliers and often decide to stock a product based on the pricing they can get.

A challenge for buyers is the huge number of new products available. Each year, about 20,000 new supermarket products are introduced. Many are made by small businesses, whose survival relies on whether they can get their new product on supermarket shelves.[5] Stores sometimes take advantage of manufacturers that

When the snack brand HighKey introduced a line of low-carb cookies, the company figured out an unconventional strategy to get it onto supermarket shelves. It paid social media influencers to promote the cookies to their large online audiences. HighKey soon had the best-selling chocolate chip cookie on the online retailer Amazon. Because of strong customer demand, supermarkets were eager to get HighKey in their stores and did not ask for any of the fees often charged to shelve new products.

are desperate for shelf space. Chain buyers might ask for a free-fill, a practice that is a high-stakes gamble for manufacturers. They have to provide large qualities of their product for no money. But if the product sells well for a chain, the stores might make the product a regular part of their inventories. Stores may also make small manufacturers pay for free-sample stations, for advertisements in the chain's newsletter, or for making an announcement about the product over the store's speaker system.

PRIVATE LABELS

Supermarkets can increase their profits by using private-label brands. These are low-priced products exclusive to chains. Stores have long sold cheap knockoffs of popular brand-name products. But in recent decades, the example of Trader Joe's has encouraged supermarkets to dedicate more shelf space to private labels, which help create a unique identity for the chain. Popular private labels include Kroger's Private Selection, Walmart's Great Value, and Target's Good & Gather.

Private labels found new customers during the early 2020s when many well-known brands raised their prices as inflation rose. In the past, shoppers had been fiercely loyal to their favorite brand names, but that loyalty eroded with the widespread belief that brands were using inflation as an excuse for hiking their prices. A 2023 survey by the Food Industry Association reported that, since 2020, 41 percent of shoppers had become more willing to try private-label products.[6]

The quality of private-label products also attracted shoppers. When supermarket chains decide to copy a brand-name product for their private-label offerings, they often contract with the same manufacturer that produces the brand-name item they are trying to imitate. As a result, cheaper private-label products are often almost indistinguishable from their brand-name counterparts. As more shoppers embrace private labels, the influence that brand-name food manufacturers have over the supermarket industry has lessened.

CHAPTER FIVE

THE PSYCHOLOGY OF SUPERMARKETS

Americans have long been suspicious about the allure of supermarkets and the effect they have on consumers' judgment. As early as 1957, social critic Vance Packard in his book *The Hidden Persuaders* sounded the alarm that the supermarket experience was turning American women into virtual zombies:

> *The ladies fell into . . . a light kind of trance that . . . is the first stage of hypnosis. . . . Interestingly many of these women were in such a trance that they passed by neighbors and old friends without noticing or greeting them. Some had a sort of glassy stare. They were so entranced as they wandered about the store plucking things off shelves at random that they would bump into boxes without seeing them.*[1]

Although Packard's depiction of entranced female shoppers might now read as absurd, there is

Supermarkets are designed to keep customers shopping
for as long as possible.

some truth to the idea that the modern supermarket can be overwhelming for customers. Researchers at Bangor University in Wales who conducted brain-scan experiments on shoppers found that after 40 minutes of grocery shopping, customers' ability to make rational choices about what they were buying decreased dramatically.

The sheer number of choices customers have to make overloads their brains so much that their emotions, rather than rational judgement, begin to dictate their purchases. Even customers who enter a supermarket with a precise list of items to purchase can end up buying products on impulse. Environmental psychologist Paco Underhill estimates that as much of 50 percent of the average supermarket customers' purchases are items they had not intended to buy when they stepped through the door.[2]

The wide array of products is just one reason supermarket shoppers tend to overbuy. Chains also have developed strategies to keep customers in their stores for as long as possible, knowing that the longer they shop, the more they are likely to buy. Music playing over the sound system soothes shoppers, so they are less likely to grab just the items on their lists and quickly head to the checkout. Slight bumpy surfaces on aisle floors also help to slow down customers. Most supermarkets have few clocks, windows, and skylights, so customers are less likely notice the passage of time.

DESIGNED TO SELL

The very architecture of supermarkets helps keep customers shopping. The most popular design features a racetrack-like outer section surrounding a rectangle of aisles known to experts as center store. As customers enter, the store design often subtly steers them to move on a counterclockwise route. It feels natural to many people to move toward the right of the store after entering, simply because most people are right-handed.

The produce section is generally the first department customers encounter. The lighting is carefully calibrated to make the fruit and vegetables to look most appealing. They are often shelved against a black background to

Grocery stores often wax apples to give them a shiny and fresh look.

make the produce's bright colors pop. Mists of water coat the vegetables, not to preserve them, but to make them look as if they are covered in dew, which gives the impression that they are freshly picked.

Next, customers see a display of plants and cut flowers. The flower section is a relatively new addition to supermarkets and adds little to the bottom line, accounting for just 1.4 percent of all sales.[3] But it does contribute to the sensory display of the produce section. The bright colors and smells of the produce and flowers together give an impression of freshness, putting customers in a good mood as they begin their shopping trip.

Shoppers then come upon the in-store bakery, where the warm air gives them a sense of coziness. The smell of freshly baked bread relaxes customers, which may make them more susceptible to buying on impulse. Pleasant food smells also trigger the sense of taste, making shoppers think about how much they would enjoy eating the products they see around them.

DAIRY, MEATS, AND FISH

Toward the back of the store is the dairy department. Originally, it was placed there to force customers to move through the entire store on the assumption that milk was bound to be on every shopping list. Milk consumption has dropped considerably, but the dairy case remains in this position, largely because other products in the dairy section, such as yogurt and milk substitutes, have grown in popularity.

Also found in the back of most supermarkets are the meat and seafood departments. The meat displayed is precut and packaged in trays covered with plastic wrap. The tidy display is designed to hide any evidence of the

TOO MUCH FOOD

When shoppers enter a supermarket, they want to see shelves that are fully stocked and produce bins that are full of fruits and vegetables. But that expectation comes at a cost. Supermarkets have to order more goods than they can sell to keep the store fully stocked at all times, an expense that is passed on to customers in the form of higher prices. Stores also have to throw away unsold food that goes bad or is past its expiration date, leading to an enormous amount of food waste.

butchering process, which many customers do not want to think about. The seafood counter is carefully monitored to reduce any fishy smell that might put off shoppers. The fresh seafood is often displayed on crushed ice to suggest freshness.

CENTER STORE

In center store, customers encounter aisle after aisle stocked with boxes, cans, and bottles. These are mostly branded products—including soups, cereals, cake mixes, condiments, beans, spices, chips, and soda—that have a long shelf life, unlike the perishables along the outer sections of the store.

Often much of the shelf space is taken up with multiple different versions of the same product. For example, a single brand of potato chips might be available with a wide variety of flavors—from barbeque to sour cream and onion to salt and vinegar. It is relatively inexpensive for food manufacturers to add numerous flavors to a core product to create these varieties.

Food companies make these additional products because of what they call "brand extension," which entails crowding other brands out of that section of the supermarket. In addition, by placing all the products together on a shelf, they create a "billboard effect." The eye-catching display acts as an advertisement for further customer awareness of the brand.

SLOTTING FEES

For many chains, center store is a major profit center because manufacturers pay stores slotting fees to have their products shelved in the best locations. Slotting fees can be very expensive. For instance, promoting a product in prime shelf space for several weeks might cost a food company as much as $300,000.[5] Without these fees, some supermarkets would not make enough revenue to stay in business.

The supermarket industry identifies the best shelf space as "between eye and thigh," according to food marketing professor John Stanton.[6] Customers tend to buy products they can easily see, so manufacturers will pay to have their products shelved at eye level. Industry insiders often advise customers seeking deals to check the tops and bottoms of shelves. These locations are filled with bargain products

made by food companies without the marketing dollars to pay for better placement.

Slotting fees are highest in the sections of stores where shelf space is limited. For example, ice cream brands pay a premium because stores have only so many freezers. Food companies with large marketing budgets can also bid to have a product named the category captain. That product's manufacturer can then dictate how all the items in a particular section are arranged. A brand with a category captain can sideline competitors' products.

Food companies are also willing to pay to have products shelved on endcaps. Products displayed there sell about eight times faster than those shelved on center store aisles.[7]

The shelves along checkout lanes are also prime locations. Candy, magazines, and other items placed there sell especially well. Customers waiting in line often succumb to these tempting impulse buys.

HIGH-VALUE SHOPPERS

While slotting fees remain a major portion of supermarket revenue, stores are increasingly waiving those fees for certain products. Using new and better customer data, stores can now identify the types of shoppers who are likely to spend the most money.

These high-value customers often want to buy products from small local brands and prefer foods with fewer processed ingredients. Attracting these customers is very profitable. Many supermarkets are happy to give away prime real estate in their stores for free to the specialty brands these shoppers prefer.

THE THANKSGIVING RUSH

Supermarkets are at their most crowded on the Tuesday before Thanksgiving. Shoppers try to beat the shopping rush by going on Tuesday rather than Wednesday, which they wrongly assume is the biggest food shopping day of the year. In fact, the Wednesday before Thanksgiving is comparatively uncrowded because most shoppers then are just picking up one or two ingredients for their holiday dinner that they had previously forgotten to buy.

CHAPTER SIX

ISSUES WITH MODERN SUPERMARKETS

A social media post by Nathalie Gordon set off a Twitter firestorm on March 3, 2016: "If only nature would find a way to cover these oranges so we didn't need to waste so much plastic on them." The message was accompanied by a photograph showing a shelf at a Whole Foods Market filled with plastic boxes, each with a single peeled Sumo tangerine inside, on sale for $5.99 a pound.[1] Quickly, the tweet received thousands of responses from people both amused and outraged by Whole Foods' assumption that its customers would pay a premium just to avoid the inconvenience of having to peel a piece of fruit themselves.

The backlash was so strong that, within hours, Whole Foods felt it necessary to respond. The company tweeted, "These have been pulled. We hear you, and we will leave them in their natural

Fruits and vegetables that are cut and sold in plastic containers may be convenient for consumers, but the extra packaging is not good for the environment.

At many supermarkets, whole vegetables are sold in plastic cartons or wrapping in an effort to keep them fresh. Most of this plastic ends up in the trash instead of being recycled.

packaging: the peel."[2] As this brief social media dust-up revealed, supermarkets are sometimes eager to address customer complaints, especially if they go viral online. But chains are often less responsive to more significant criticisms of the ways their business practices have an adverse effect on their customers and society at large.

In recent years, nutritionists, environmentalists, financial experts, privacy advocates, and customers themselves have pressed the supermarket industry to make changes to its business model, usually with only limited success.

PACKAGING WASTE

Among these critics was Gordon, who in an interview with CBS News, took pains to make sure her broader point was not lost during the Sumo tangerine kerfuffle. As she explained, "Whole Foods has an unhealthy relationship with plastic, and I think they need to address that as a wider point."[3] Supermarkets have often come under fire for the waste created by excess packaging. Packaging accounts for about one-quarter of all trash found in landfills across the United States.[4]

Plastic packaging, particularly prevalent in the supermarket industry, is seen as especially damaging. Plastic is made from fossil fuels, so its manufacture contributes to the growing problems associated with climate change. Health professionals and scientists are also concerned about the effects of exposure to plastic on the human body. They are especially interested in how plastic packaging might contaminate foods and beverages people routinely consume.

Supermarkets have often promoted recycling as a remedy to plastic waste. But for decades, the recycling rate of plastic waste in the United States has been low, remaining at just under 6 percent.[5] For environmentalists, the more obvious answer to the problem of supermarket plastic waste is to remove it from grocery shelves altogether.

GETTING RID OF PLASTICS

Financially, supermarkets have little incentive to go plastic-free. Plastic is a cheap material, and because it is light, it is cheaper to transport than glass or other similar

ZERO-WASTE SUPERMARKETS

At Precycle in Brooklyn, New York, customers carry their groceries home in reusable containers they brought to the store or purchased there. It is a zero-waste supermarket, a store designed to eliminate all excess packaging from the grocery shopping experience. During the 2010s, zero-waste supermarkets began popping up in European cities such as London, England; Berlin, Germany; Amsterdam, the Netherlands; and Stockholm, Sweden. Although mostly small-scale operations, individual zero-waste stores are now found throughout the world.

packing materials. There is also another important practical reason for plastic packaging in supermarkets. It is very effective in slowing the decay of produce and other perishables. For this reason, getting rid of plastic packaging actually risks substantially increasing food waste.

Nevertheless, several countries, including many in Europe, have taken measures to reduce plastic packaging. For instance, Spain has a plastic tax to reduce use, and France has placed limits on packaging produce in plastic. Canada has plans to eliminate almost all plastic packaging by 2028.

The United States has been relatively slow to take action on plastic waste. However, by 2024, 12 states had placed some restrictions on plastic packaging. Some food retailers have also made policies to address the problem.

John Mackey

During his 44-year tenure as chief executive officer of Whole Foods Market, John Mackey helped make organic and natural foods part of the typical American diet. Born in 1953, Mackey grew up in Houston, Texas. When he was 25, he borrowed money from family and friends to open a small health food store. Two years later, he merged his business with another company and established the first Whole Foods in Austin, Texas.

In the 1990s, Whole Foods went national as Mackey oversaw its acquisition of health food stores throughout the United States. Mackey's company set high standards for the products it sold, forcing food manufacturers it did business with to eliminate artificial flavors, coloring, and preservatives from their products. The chain's buying power also compelled meat companies to adhere to its strict guidelines for organic foods. Mackey became a leading force in the promotion of humane living conditions for livestock.

Whole Foods' success also changed the grocery industry. Mackey proved that there existed a high customer demand for organic and natural foods. As a result, other supermarkets began stocking more of these products. In 2017, Amazon purchased Whole Foods for $13.7 billion.[6] After leaving the company in 2022, Mackey founded a health-care business called Love.Life and published a memoir titled *The Whole Story*.

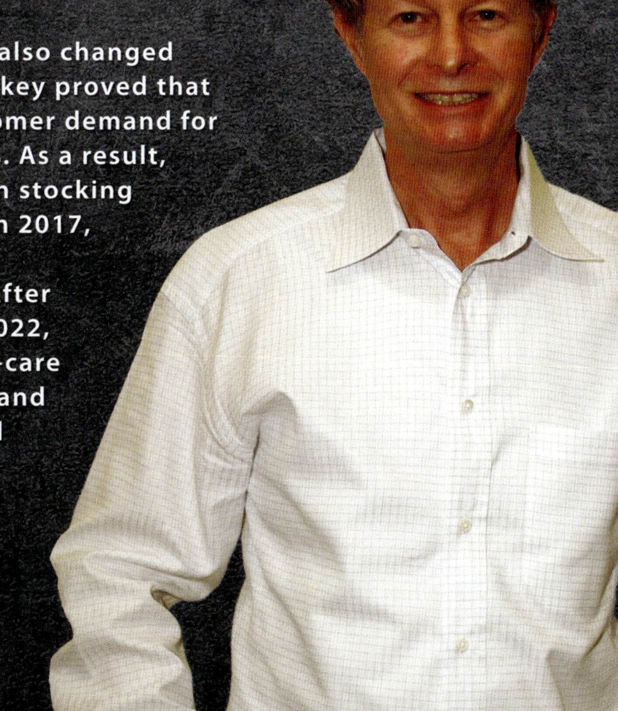

Plastic grocery bags harm the environment. In the United States, 12 states and more than 500 cities have placed a ban on using plastic bags in grocery stores.

Walmart and Costco, for instance, are working to ensure that the plastic packaging for products in their house brands is fully recyclable. Kroger has phased out the use of plastic bags. In the past, the chain used about six billion plastic bags annually—enough to fill more than 3,000 moving trucks.[7]

The supermarket industry is also pressing for food packaging that is less harmful to the environment. Some ideas include making bags from beechwood trees, cellophane-like film using orange peels and shrimp shells, and trays and boxes from rice paddy straw and sugar cane stalks. Unlike plastic, all these types of packaging would be biodegradable.

ULTRA-PROCESSED FOODS

Many activists have complaints not only about food packaging in supermarkets but also with the food itself. They are particularly concerned with ultra-processed foods—products usually found in stores' center aisles, such as frozen meals, instant soups, jarred sauces, packaged cookies, soft drinks, and potato chips.

Only a small number of foods sold in supermarkets are completely unprocessed. Eggs and avocados, for instance, are virtually unchanged as they move from the farm to the grocery. More products are minimally processed, meaning they were slightly altered during manufacturing through cooking, fermenting, or some other process. Milk, for example, is pasteurized before it reaches the supermarket refrigeration case so that it doesn't spoil as quickly. The natural ingredients in ultra-processed foods, however, are transformed by manufacturers using additives, preservatives, emulsifiers, and artificial coloring and flavors, creating what food writer Michael Pollan calls "edible foodlike substances."[8]

Cheap to produce, ultra-processed foods are attractive to supermarkets because they have a long shelf life. But most ultra-processed foods are unhealthy because they contain large amounts of sugar, fat, and salt. Overconsumption of

IS PROCESSING FOOD UNHEALTHY?

Ultra-processed foods are often seen as unhealthy because they contain high amounts of salt, sugar, and saturated fats. But some scientists are studying whether processing itself makes these foods harmful to the body. For instance, studies show that when ultra-processed foods containing ground nuts are consumed, the body absorbs more of the nuts' fat in comparison to eating whole nuts. Another theory holds that emulsifiers, used to mix ingredients in ultra-processed foods, cause overeating because they interfere with gut microbes that give people a feeling of fullness.

these products has been linked to health problems such as high blood pressure, type 2 diabetes, and dementia.

Despite these health risks, supermarket shoppers readily buy ultra-processed foods, which account for more than half of the calories consumed by Americans. Customers are attracted to ultra-processed foods because of their low cost and convenience. But they are also influenced by aggressive marketing by food manufacturers. Many marketing campaigns are deceptive as they try to imply that these harmful foods are actually healthy choices.

MINING DATA

Many supermarket customers sign up for loyalty programs, which reward frequent shoppers with discounts and even the occasional free gift. To enroll, customers provide chains with personal information, such as their name, address, email, and birthday. Most think surrendering this information is a small price to pay for the customized coupons stores give them in exchange.

But largely without customers' knowledge, supermarket chains are increasingly selling information about their shoppers to third parties, including food manufacturers, so they can use the data to market their products. Supermarkets get additional information by using cameras to track customers' movements through their stores. Online orders also provide a digital record of customers' past purchases and preferences.

From this information, stores can compile profiles of customers that include information about their race, ethnicity, age, finances, employment, online activities, and health status. Surveillance experts decry the collection and sale of this data as a serious invasion of privacy. But, increasingly, supermarket chains are relying on data collection as an important source of revenue. For instance, the large chain Kroger, at which 60 million households regularly shop, operates its own data science unit as part of its "alternative profit business," which the chain expects to eventually bring in more than $1 billion a year.[10]

CHAIN MEGAMERGERS

Kroger's customer base is only likely to grow. In 2022, the chain announced plans to acquire the Albertsons chain for $24.6 billion. Under the merger, Kroger would operate 5,000 stores.[11] This would mean the chain would control about 22 percent of the food retail market.[12] Recent decades have seen other such megamergers in the supermarket industry. Albertsons merged with the Safeway supermarket chain in 2015. In 2017, online retailer Amazon bought Whole Foods, and in 2024, the Germany-based chain ALDI purchased Winn-Dixie, a major chain in the southeastern United States.

In the industry, these mergers were seen a response to Walmart's entry into the grocery business. The buying power of the discount giant allowed it to demand steep price reductions from food suppliers. Other chains merged into larger companies to help them get similar discounts in order to compete with Walmart.

Regulators at the Federal Trade Commission are seeking to block the Kroger-Albertsons merger, saying that the merger would be bad for consumers because it would allow the chain to raise prices. For instance, before the proposed merger, a Kroger and an Albertsons located near one another would compete to offer shoppers the best price

Together, the Kroger and Albertsons companies control 39 grocery brands.

on their goods. But if the two companies merge, a lack of nearby competition could lead those two stores to charge higher prices.

FOOD DESERTS

Mergers also often result in corporations closing underperforming stores. Not only do employees of these stores lose their jobs but communities lose the benefit of having a nearby supermarket. Losing a supermarket can be especially devastating to low-income neighborhoods that run the risk of becoming food deserts.

Food deserts are communities without a nearby supermarket where people can buy fresh, healthy foods.

Buses loaded with groceries provide access to nutritious food for people living in small towns in Germany. The same concept has been used to serve food deserts in US cities such as Minneapolis, Minnesota.

A 2017 report estimated that about 30 million Americans live in food deserts.[13] For low-income households without a car or other reliable means of transportation, buying fresh food becomes difficult, if not impossible. People may have to rely on unhealthy fast food and on ultra-processed products on sale at convenience stores. This poor diet leaves them more susceptible to chronic health conditions, such as type 2 diabetes and heart disease.

Federal and local governments have provided funds to food businesses to encourage them to open stores in food deserts. Between 2004 and 2016, more than

1,000 supermarkets were established in these areas.[14] But a 2019 study published in the *Quarterly Journal of Economics* suggested that establishing a local supermarket in a former food desert does not necessarily discourage nearby residents from purchasing and consuming a diet heavy in ultra-processed foods. Low income households are like all Americans in that even when they are given more healthy options, they still often buy the processed foods the food industry markets so successfully.

SAVING A SUPERMARKET

In 2023, the owner of the only full-service grocery store in the small, rural town of Sheffield, Illinois, was about to retire. Not wanting to travel 15 miles (24 km) to the next nearest supermarket to get their groceries, Sheffield residents came up with a unique solution. They pooled their funds and collected enough money to buy the store. Now run by a nonprofit group, the renovated store not only allows the people of Sheffield to get groceries close to home but also functions as a community center.

CHAPTER SEVEN

COVID-19 AND ONLINE SHOPPING

By mid-March 2020, grocery shopping became something it had never been before: dangerous. As the COVID-19 pandemic spread worldwide, Americans were advised to stay home as much as possible to avoid getting infected. For many, the only time they ventured out was for a trip to the supermarket.

Suddenly, the supermarket experience seemed entirely new. Following health experts' guidelines, many customers wore face coverings as they wandered the aisles. They doused their hands in sanitizer and cleaned their carts' handles with disinfectant wipes. Nervously, shoppers struggled to get everything they needed quickly, all while trying to stay at least the recommended six feet (1.8 m) away from anyone else.[1]

Shoppers wore masks to the grocery store early in the
COVID-19 pandemic.

FOOD AT A DISCOUNT

The Flashfood app helps eliminate food waste while offering users big deals on groceries. It identifies meat, produce, dairy, and other perishable products at nearby supermarkets that are slightly overripe or nearing their expiration dates. Shoppers can use the app to buy these items at a steep discount and then go to the supermarket to pick up their bagged purchases.

But perhaps the oddest thing customers had to deal with was empty shelves picked clean of merchandise. The pandemic had disrupted supply chains worldwide, keeping many products from even reaching supermarkets. Panicked shoppers also hoarded certain necessities, such as toilet paper, depleting stores' supplies. Americans were so accustomed to supermarkets fully stocked with products that empty grocery shelves became a symbol of just how much the pandemic had turned everyday life upside down.

WORKING FOR CHANGE

As the pandemic stretched on, it began to change grocery shopping habits. To get out of the supermarket as soon as possible, many customers began to rely on tried-and-true products, decreasing new product sales and impulse buys. With restaurant dining areas closed or restricted, spending in supermarkets went up, and some people took up cooking as a new hobby. As supply chain problems led to inflation, many customers spent more of their grocery budgets on low-cost store brands. The pandemic also accelerated several trends that were already reshaping the supermarket industry.

Before the pandemic, many supermarket employees were dissatisfied with their working conditions. Looking to cut costs, many chains paid workers low wages, and most employees did not belong to a union that could negotiate for higher pay. Often, employees were unable to get enough hours of work a week to make a living wage. They were also unable to get a second job because their employers would not provide them with a consistent schedule. Sometimes, chains promised workers benefits, such as health insurance, that few employees actually received.

When the pandemic hit, many Americans started working from home. But supermarket employees, unable to do their jobs remotely, were deemed essential workers and therefore expected to report to work. Despite the risks of working in an enclosed space crowded with fellow employees and customers, some grocery workers did not receive protective gear from their employers. The United Food and Commercial Workers International Union, whose members include supermarket employees, reported 29,000 of its frontline workers were infected or exposed to COVID-19 during a 100-day period from April through June of 2020. About 238 union members died from the disease during that period.[2]

Some supermarket employees quit their jobs because of how they were treated during the pandemic. Others began organizing to improve their pay and working conditions. With leverage from labor shortages, many grocery workers have since organized strikes or joined unions to demand better pay and working conditions.

ONLINE SHOPPING

By 2020, online ordering made up a large percentage of retailers' business for most products. For instance, about 50 percent of books, 40 percent of consumer electronics, and 30 percent of clothing purchases were made online. Online shopping, however, was still only a tiny share of the grocery market. Only 3 percent of grocery sales were made online.[3]

During the pandemic, that changed very quickly. Afraid of contracting COVID-19 at the supermarket, many shoppers turned to the internet to get their weekly groceries.

Empty shelves became a problem at grocery stores around the world as COVID-19 caused supply chain shortages.

Amazon, which had purchased Whole Foods in 2017, suddenly had 50 times more online grocery delivery orders and had to hire 175,000 employees to handle the workload. Other chains also scrambled to improve their online delivery systems. Third-party delivery services such as Instacart worked with supermarkets to get these orders to consumers. The company hired 300,000 new workers to go to supermarkets to assemble online orders and deliver them.[4]

In 2019, before the pandemic, chains such as Walmart, Kroger, and Safeway started offering pickup services. A customer could place a grocery order online, drive to the store, and park in a designated pickup space. After assembling the order, an employee then delivered the groceries to the trunk of the customer's car, eliminating face-to-face contact. To further protect grocery workers, some supermarkets established what were called dark stores. Not open to the public, dark stores were used solely to put together online orders.

IN-STORE AND ONLINE

In a matter of months, online grocery shopping went from something only a few people had ever considered to a commonplace method of buying food. By July 2021, about 10 percent of grocery orders were placed online. An estimated 60 percent of American adults had ordered groceries on the internet at least once.[5]

For both supermarkets and customers, online grocery orders had obvious downsides. Internet shopping eliminated many of the impulse buys supermarkets rely on for revenue. The job of picking up products and placing them in a cart had traditionally been performed by customers for free. With online ordering,

Online ordering through traditional grocery stores and through online-only retailers became popular options during the height of the pandemic.

that task was now performed by a paid employee of a supermarket or a third-party service. With the additional labor costs for delivery orders, the price of online orders was higher than in-store purchases.

Many customers also disliked the idea of someone else choosing their perishable purchases, such as fresh produce and meat. To satisfy these shoppers, some supermarkets have created a new business model that integrates online and in-store shopping. Before going to the store, customers can place an online order for packaged staples from the supermarket's center aisles, such as paper towels, canned vegetables, and cereal. At a mini warehouse in the back of the store, the order is prepared. When the customer arrives to pick it up, the shopper can first roam the fresh-food sections to select items on their own.

SHOPPING WITH TECHNOLOGY

As the worst of the pandemic wound down, supermarkets were eager to lure customers back to their stores. Many fully embraced technological innovations to improve the in-store experience. The most common uses of new technology in American supermarkets are smartphone apps that allow customers to order groceries for delivery or pickup.

LARGEST FOOD RETAILERS IN NORTH AMERICA BY SALES, 2023[6]

Among food retailer giants, Walmart has the largest share of the market, with almost twice the sales of Amazon, the second-largest food retailer.

*sales from online and physical stores

Some apps let users build shopping lists of items they regularly purchase or access a favorite recipe and quickly order all the ingredients they do not have on hand. Many shoppers also use online coupons customized for members of supermarket chains' loyalty programs.

At the same time, some chains, such as Walmart and Costco, are looking at how to improve an older technological advance—the self-checkout. A fixture in retail stores for decades, the self-checkout has long frustrated both supermarket customers and employees. Although intended to reduce time at the checkout, self-checkouts often made waits longer because customers scan and bag their purchases more slowly than trained cashiers do. The technology is also glitchy, requiring shoppers to flag down an employee to help them when a machine malfunctions.

Supermarkets originally adopted self-checkout so they could hire fewer workers. In addition to hurting employees' morale, the reductions in staff left many stores messier, with rows of shelves unstocked. Self-checkout also reduced revenue because shoppers often incorrectly scanned their purchases. Additionally, some customers take advantage of the opportunity for easier shoplifting.

IMPROVING THE SUPERMARKET EXPERIENCE

Another way some supermarkets have tried to improve their in-store experience is by accommodating shoppers with sensory processing disorders. For people with autism, attention deficit hyperactivity disorder, and traumatic brain injuries, the bright fluorescent lights and loud announcements over speaker systems can be extremely stressful. Walmart is experimenting with sensory-friendly shopping hours, during which the lights are dimmed and any music or announcements are quiet.

Supermarkets have long touted the incredible variety

OMEGA MART

Even people who find grocery shopping boring might be excited by Omega Mart. Opened in February 2021 in Las Vegas, Nevada, this huge installation created by hundreds of artists allows visitors to explore a fake supermarket full of weird invented products such as Organic Moth Milk and Lil Meow Gruel for Cats, which came in Pigeon Mousse flavor. Omega Mart is a portal to a series of immersive multimedia exhibits with elaborate lighting and sound designs and full of video and digital content. An estimated one million people experience Omega Mart each year.[8]

of products they sell. But some innovative stores are opting to carry fewer items while thoughtfully selecting and displaying those they do stock. One such curated grocery store is Pop Up Grocer in New York City, which appeals to younger customers. Looking more like a clothing boutique than a conventional supermarket, the store showcases new and interesting products made by small businesses, with an emphasis on packaging that features attractive design.

Some supermarkets are trying to lure more shoppers by incorporating other businesses into their stores. Customers may be able to combine grocery shopping with grabbing a fast food lunch, getting a prescription, or having a spa treatment. By offering a location for one-stop shopping, these stores are trying to take the place of shopping malls. Supermarkets are even adding bars and restaurants, inviting shoppers to stay and hang out with friends.

SLOW CHECKOUTS

The Dutch supermarket chain Jumbo offers customers an alternative to a rushed and harried checkout experience. Some of its checkouts are designated as Kletskassas ("chat checkout") lines. Shoppers in these checkout lines are encouraged to take their time and strike up a conversation with the cashier. Now found in some other European supermarkets, slow checkouts are popular with retirees and stay-at-home parents who enjoy having more social interaction during their grocery trips.

CHAPTER EIGHT

SUPERMARKETS OF TOMORROW

A shopper enters his favorite supermarket and begins to roam its aisles. He picks up a jar of tomato sauce. He immediately sees a read-out of nutritional information and recipe suggestions floating in midair beside it. As he puts it in his cart, a store employee appears in his field of view and suggests he pair the sauce with a new brand of mushroom ravioli because he frequently buys mushrooms.

The customer adds the ravioli to his cart and heads for the dairy aisle. When he unthinkingly reaches for a gallon (3.8 L) of milk, another employee appears. She reminds him he bought milk a few days ago and still has most of a jug in his refrigerator. The customer thanks her and collects the rest of the items he needs. When he is finished, he reviews a list

In the not-so-distant future, shoppers may be able to use virtual reality or augmented reality to do their grocery shopping.

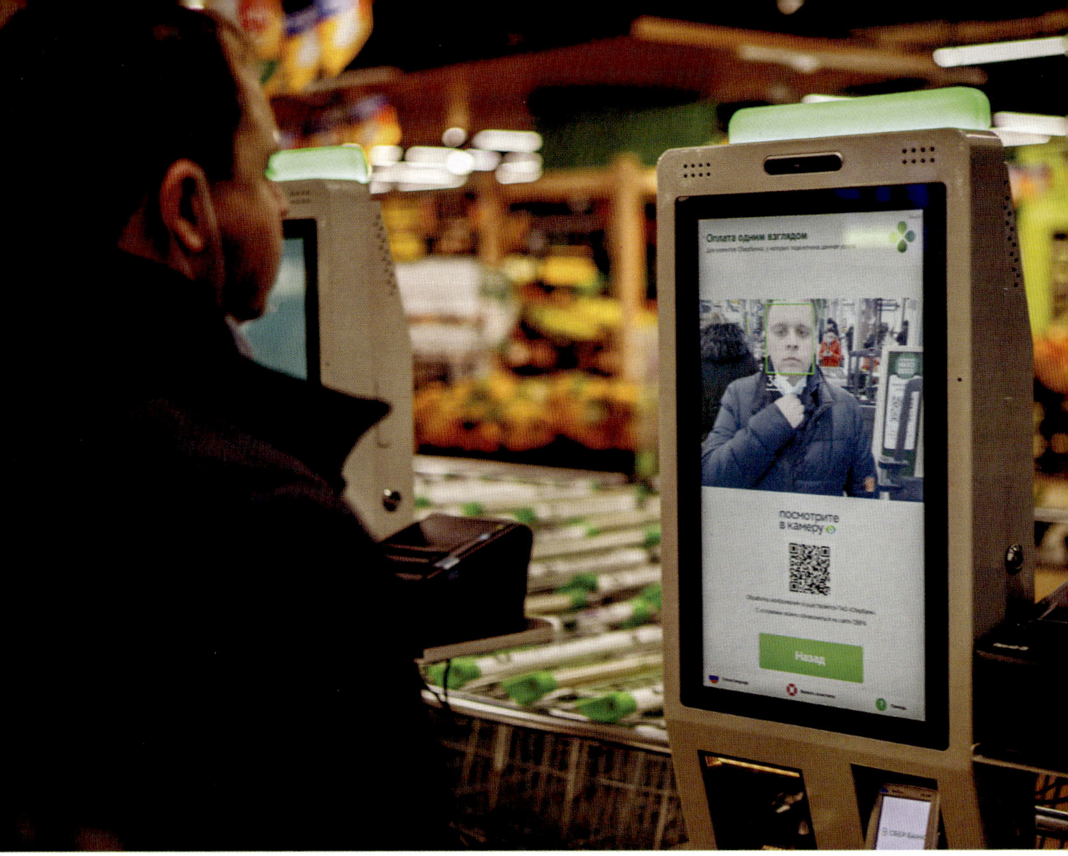

In some countries, facial recognition is used in supermarkets to pay at self-checkout machines.

of his purchases that appears before his eyes and checks out in an instant.

The shopper then pulls off his virtual reality (VR) headset. He is no longer in a supermarket but in his living room, sitting on the couch, waiting for his grocery order to be delivered. Through VR technology, he had the experience of shopping in a store without ever leaving his home. The idea of buying groceries in a VR setting might sound like science fiction, but scenarios like this are becoming possible with modern technology. This is just one way supermarket

shopping in the future may be transformed through new
and evolving technologies.

ARTIFICIAL INTELLIGENCE

Artificial intelligence (AI), a term used to describe computer
systems that can perform tasks usually associated with
human intelligence, will likely soon play an important role in
the supermarket industry. One possible use of AI is to answer
customers' questions. It may also be employed to market
new products to customers based on past purchases and to
alert them to sale items they may interested in.

Because many shoppers are willing to pay more for
products that promote health and wellness, AI may also
guide shoppers toward healthy food choices based on
their own medical records. A 2023 study of 2,000 grocery
customers, however, found that many people were wary of
AI systems. Only 22 percent trusted their grocery store to use
the technology responsibly.[1]

AI will probably be most important behind the scenes,
helping supermarkets manage supply-chain logistics—a
notoriously difficult task. The technology could oversee
store inventories and negotiate directly with suppliers. Other
uses of AI include helping select private-label products

based on customer data and functioning as a company spokesperson on social media accounts.

A more controversial technology finding its way into supermarkets is facial recognition software. This tool, which can recognize people by their facial features, is being used to combat shoplifting. If a person steals something, the system could make it easier to identify them. Later in the COVID-19 pandemic, when many retailers had seen an uptick in theft, facial recognition software was adopted by more supermarkets in the United States, often against the objections of privacy advocates. In 2023, New York City grocers fought hard against a privacy bill considered by the city council. The bill would ban the facial recognition software unless stores posted a notice that stated they were using it and obtained written consent from their customers.

CHECKING OUT

New technologies are also being adopted to improve the supermarket checkout experience. Not all of these efforts succeed, such as when Amazon experimented with eliminating checkouts altogether. In its Amazon Fresh stores, customers could grab snacks, beverages, and meals and simply walk out the door. The stores were outfitted with elaborate sensors and cameras assisted by machine learning that would monitor which items customers took and bill shoppers' credit cards directly. Amazon spent $1 million to outfit each Fresh location with what it called "Just Walk Out" technology.[2] But in 2024, the company announced it was removing the technology from its Fresh stores. News reports revealed that the system had required about 1,000 employees, most based in India, to monitor the supposedly automated Just Walk Out transactions.[3]

Another option for frictionless checkout is scan-and-go technology, which allows customers to pay for their purchase by scanning product barcodes using their smartphones. Walmart and Wegmans adopted this system briefly but have largely abandoned it. Many customers resented having to do the job of a cashier, and chains complained about lost revenue from items that were

MARTY THE ROBOT

At more than 300 stores in the Stop & Shop chain, Marty the Robot roams the aisles.[4] The robot monitors the shelves, alerting staff to misplaced items and products that need restocking. He also looks for spills on the floor that pose a safety hazard. But perhaps Marty's most important role is as an ambassador for the store brand. Beloved by customers, he frequently appears at local charity and sporting events.

left unscanned by customers, either inadvertently or
on purpose.

Smart carts are proving to be a more successful means
of bypassing checkout lines. Some smart carts are outfitted
with cameras and scales to record purchases, with a video
display showing customers a running tally of the price of
the items in their cart. Portable units that can transform
traditional carts into smart carts are more affordable. At
select Wegmans stores, customers can pick up units from a
charging station, attach them to their carts, and leave with
their bagged purchases without having to stop at a cashier
or self-checkout.

At a chain called Seven Fresh in China, shoppers can
use a more elaborate smart cart. In addition to totaling
purchases, these robotic carts move on their own without
being pushed. The robots follow the customer as they
wander through the store, controlled by a tracking device
the customer wears on their wrist.

ROBOTS AT WORK

Advances in robotics are changing supermarkets in
several ways. In 2018, Kroger began investing in enormous
fulfillment centers where robots help assemble orders

for delivery. Within these massive warehouses, a team of more than 1,000 robots, each about the size of a dishwasher, meander over a vast grid called the Hive.[5] Here, about 31,000 different grocery items are stored.[6] After a robot retrieves the items for an order, it delivers them to a station where employees bag and load

Starship robots park outside participating supermarkets, ready to deliver orders to customers. Starship service is available in 60 locations around the world, including on many US college campuses.

orders onto waiting trucks. Originally, Kroger planned to have 20 robotic fulfillment centers in operation within three years. But by 2023, only eight had been opened.[7] The cost of setting up each warehouse was $55 million.[8]

Kroger, Save Mart, and other chains are also experimenting with delivering online orders by robot. The tech company Starship has created six-wheeled delivery robots. Each robotic vehicle can carry about three bags of groceries in its trunk, which customers can open with an app on their smartphone. During tests on college campuses, the vehicles have been able to navigate curbs and cross streets without the help of humans.

CULTIVATED MEAT

More than 100 tech companies are now working on the same problem: how to get cultivated meat on grocery shelves. Cultivated meat is grown in a laboratory from a few cells of a living animal, but it is too expensive to make to sell commercially. An expert estimated in 2020 that producing one pound (0.45 kg) of cultivated meat costs about $17, meaning it would be sold for about $40 a pound in a supermarket. However, Eat Just, the first company to sell cultivated chicken, predicts that its product will cost the same as traditional chicken meat by 2030.[10]

Drones pose another possible way to deliver groceries. Several chains have worked with Deuce Drone, whose drones can carry up to ten pounds (4.5 kg) of groceries and drop them outside customers' homes.[9] Even if drone technology improves enough to make these systems economically viable, they may still prove impractical because of local laws and regulations regarding flying vehicles.

For decades, the grocery industry has been anticipating autonomous trucks that could move products from warehouses to retail stores. Driverless trucks would not only save on labor costs but they could also run 24 hours a day, while regulations restrict human drivers to working no more than 11 hours at a stretch. Although the development of the technology has been slow, Kroger was able to begin a test program in north Texas in 2023. During the test, small autonomous trucks transported frozen food from a Dallas warehouse to three retail locations in the area. Each truck, however, traveled with a safety driver aboard who could take control if needed, helping ensure the trucks were able to navigate highways and roads successfully.

GROWING LOCALLY

In 2020, the supermarket industry was rocked when the COVID-19 pandemic disrupted the global food supply chain. But experts looking at the industry's long-term future know that an unexpected disease is not the only reason that grocery stores shelves might suddenly become bare. Wars and international trade restrictions can also restrict the flow of foreign goods. Another problem is climate change, which is likely to increase extreme weather that could kill crops unexpectedly. Climate change will also reduce the amount of farmable land and change the areas where various crops can grow.

Greenhouses have become a reliable source for locally grown produce in cities and rural areas.

The effects of climate change suggest that the current system of buying produce from around the world to stock the shelves of American supermarkets is not viable in the long term. Many American consumers also oppose this practice because of the pollution emissions that result from shipping food thousands of miles. They prefer food that is grown locally, not on a farm in a faraway country.

To deal with the looming climate crisis and customer demands, many groceries are looking to buy local produce grown using unconventional methods. Recent technology has greatly improved ways of producing crops in greenhouses. Hydroponics, the growing of produce in water rather than soil, has also become more viable and popular. For example, a hydroponic company called Sunset Produce provides Canadians with fresh strawberries even during the country's harsh winters.

VERTICAL FARMING

Another promising agricultural breakthrough is vertical farming, in which plants are grown indoors on vertically

stacked layers. Vertical farming requires no pesticides
and little water and allows crops to grow year-round.
One downside is that vertical farming uses a great deal of
energy, although innovators
in the field are working
to make systems more
energy efficient.

One of the most
successful vertical farming
companies is Bowery, a New
York City company that sells
greens to supermarkets
across the United States.
The company's software
uses sensors to constantly

One form of hydroponics uses vertical tubes filled with water as a way to grow lettuce using less space.

monitor its plants to collect data on individual plants' color,
size, and health. Machine learning systems then use that
data to control the light, water, and nutrients given to plants
to ensure the maximum yield.

Such modern advances have led many supermarkets
to explore ways to buy local produce from greenhouses,
vertical farming operations, or other options. In a 2023
survey, seven out of ten grocery executives said they

VERY LOCAL PRODUCE

A Whole Foods Market in Brooklyn, New York, takes the idea of locally grown food to the extreme. Some of its produce is cultivated in a greenhouse on the store's roof. Lettuces, herbs, and tomatoes from the rooftop hydroponic farm operated by Gotham Greens are transported to the supermarket not by truck but by elevator.

wanted to sell more locally produced foods in the future.[12] As the costs for unconventional farming techniques decrease, some supermarkets are even investigating ways to grow their own produce.

AN UNCERTAIN FUTURE

The supermarket industry today struggles with many challenges, perhaps more than at any other time in its history. Supermarkets continue to face enormous competition as more and more nontraditional food retailers are trying to capture their customers' dollars. At the same time, their already small profit margin is being eroded as they adopt expensive new technologies. Just as supermarket chains once drove independently owned stores out of business, traditional chains are now threatened by companies such as Amazon and Walmart, which have the money to more easily invest in these technologies.

Supermarkets are also heading into a future in which it is extremely hard to predict what the next generation of consumers will want and need. In their golden age during the 1950s and 1960s, supermarkets' mission was clear—providing a wide variety of foods at a low price. Their average customers were also narrowly defined, with supermarkets adapting their stores and inventories to appeal to suburban families. Now supermarket customers are much more diverse in terms of household size, racial and ethnic makeup, and food preferences. Supermarkets that try to appeal to everyone could easily find themselves providing a shopping experience that does not appeal strongly to anyone.

Online orders remain a relatively small percentage of all supermarket purchases. But over time, that could change as customers grow more comfortable buying food online and come to demand the convenience of pickup and delivery. It is possible that brick-and-mortar supermarkets themselves will become obsolete.

But given the importance of supermarkets in American life, it is difficult to imagine they will ever completely disappear. Although at times grocery shopping may seem like a chore, it is still a regular ritual for millions of Americans. It is a chance for people to take a moment out of their day to come together with others in their community and select the foods that will sustain themselves and their loved ones.

SUPERMARKET HISTORY

- In the early 1900s, Americans bought their groceries from general stores, where clerks assembled orders from lists of goods provided by customers.

- Clarence Saunders upended the grocery industry in 1916 when his Piggly Wiggly store became the first self-service grocer.

- Michael Cullen is credited with inventing the supermarket when he opened the first King Kullen store in 1930.

- In the years following World War II, the United States' supermarkets became a symbol of the country's prosperity.

- By the 1960s, supermarket chains, which could compete better on prices, had driven most independently owned grocers out of business.

- With its nationwide expansion in the 1990s, Whole Foods Market proved that many supermarket customers are willing to pay a premium for natural and organic foods.

CHALLENGES AND CONTROVERSIES

- Supermarkets now face competition from nontraditional food retailers. These include warehouse clubs, specialized groceries focusing on inexpensive in-house brands, dollar stores, drugstores, and convenience stores.

- Supermarkets are challenged by a business model that provides slim profit margins.

- Environmentalists have criticized the supermarket industry for producing large amounts of packaging waste. Plastic packaging is especially prevalent in supermarkets because it helps keep perishables, such as produce and meat, fresh.

- Ultra-processed foods sold in supermarkets' center aisles are often high in salt, sugar, and fat. Their overconsumption has been linked to serious health problems.

A CHANGING INDUSTRY

- The COVID-19 pandemic greatly disrupted the supermarket industry. It accelerated several existing trends, including the unionization of supermarket workers and the popularization of online grocery orders for delivery or pickup.

- Using hydroponics, vertical farming, and other new farming methods, many supermarkets will soon be able to grow their own produce for sale.

- In the future, more supermarkets are likely to incorporate new technologies into their business. These technologies include artificial intelligence, virtual reality, and robotics.

QUOTE

"[Supermarkets] are a reflection, even symbol, of our culture, and thus a gauge of who we are . . . what we care about, what we fear, what we desire."

—*Michael Ruhlman*, Grocery: The Buying and Selling of Food in America

GLOSSARY

additive
A chemical added to food during processing to create a desired result, such as added flavoring, stabilization of ingredients, or preservation.

barcode
A machine-readable pattern of vertical lines that can be used to identify a retail product.

biodegradable
Capable of being broken down by living organisms, such as bacteria.

drone
A small remote-controlled flying machine.

endcap
A grocery display on the end of a center aisle in a supermarket.

free-fill
A quantity of a product provided to a retailer by a manufacturer for free in hope of receiving future orders.

incentive
A thing that motivates or encourages one to do something.

inventory
All the goods available for sale at a given time at a retail store.

marketing
Promoting a product or service to encourage customers to purchase it.

merger
The combination of two companies into one.

perishable
Able to spoil or decay.

pesticide
A chemical applied to crops to kill insects.

profit margin
A retailer's revenue minus its business costs.

retailer
A business that sells goods to the public.

shelf life
The length of time a product for sale remains usable or edible.

supermarket
A large self-service retail store with a wide variety of foods and household goods for sale.

supply chain
The companies, materials, and systems involved in manufacturing and delivering a type of good.

union
A workers' organization charged with negotiating pay rates with companies and otherwise looking out for the workers' interests.

virtual reality (VR)
A computer-made simulation of a physical space, usually experienced by wearing a headset or goggles.

warehouse club
A large retail store where a variety of items are sold at a discounted rate in a warehouse setting.

MORE INFORMATION

For more information on this subject, contact or visit the
following organizations:

FOOD INDUSTRY ASSOCIATION (FMI)
2345 Crystal Dr., Ste. 800
Arlington, VA 22202
fmi.org/about-us

With food retailers and manufacturers among its members, FMI
advocates for the sale of safer, healthier, and more affordable foods to
American consumers and for a stable and efficient supply chain within
the food industry.

NATIONAL SUPERMARKET ASSOCIATION
30-50 Whitestone Expy., Ste. 301
Flushing, NY 11354
nsaglobal.org

Founded in 1989, this organization supports independent supermarkets
in urban areas not served by large grocery chains.

PINK PALACE MANSION
3050 Central Ave.
Memphis, TN 38111
info@moshmemphis.com
moshmemphis.com/exhibits-collections/pink-palace-mansion

Now owned by Memphis's Museum of Science & History, the Pink Palace
Mansion was built by Clarence Saunders, founder of the Piggly Wiggly
chain. Among its exhibits is a replica of the original Piggly Wiggly store.

SOURCE NOTES

CHAPTER 1. PIGGLY WIGGLY AND KING KULLEN

1. Benjamin Lorr. *The Secret Life of Groceries: The Dark Miracle of the American Supermarket.* Avery, 2020. 26.

2. Lorr, *Secret Life of Groceries,* 26–27.

3. Kat Eschner. "The Bizarre Story of Piggly Wiggly, the First Self-Service Grocery Store." *Smithsonian,* 6 Sept. 2017, smithsonianmag.com. Accessed 16 Feb. 2024.

4. Lorr, *Secret Life of Groceries,* 30.

5. Gary Hoover. "Supermarket: One of the Most Important (And Least Known) American Inventions of All Time." *American Business History Center,* 2 Aug. 2019, americanbusinesshistory.org. Accessed 16 Feb. 2024.

6. "Our History." *King Kullen,* 2024, kingkullen.com. Accessed 16 Feb. 2024.

7. "Our History." *Piggly Wiggly,* 2024, pigglywiggly.com. Accessed 16 Feb. 2024.

8. "Our History," *King Kullen.*

9. Elliot Zwiebach. "Michael J. Cullen: 2009 SN Hall of Fame." *Supermarket News,* 7 Dec. 2009, supermarketnews.com. Accessed 16 Feb. 2024.

10. Bianca Bosker. "The Pandemic Shows Us the Genius of Supermarkets." *Atlantic,* July/Aug. 2020, theatlantic.com. Accessed 6 Feb. 2024.

11. Elliot Zwiebach. "Michael J. Cullen: 2009 SN Hall of Fame." *Supermarket News,* 7 Dec. 2009, supermarketnews.com. Accessed 16 Feb. 2024.

12. Joe Pinsker. "Grocery Stores: An American Miracle." *Atlantic,* 25 May 2017, theatlantic.com. Accessed 7 Feb. 2024.

13. Lorr, *Secret Life of Groceries,* 32–33.

14. Michael Ruhlman. *Grocery: The Buying and Selling of Food in America.* Abrams, 2017. 2.

CHAPTER 2. SAVINGS AND VARIETY

1. Scott Allen. "'Wonderful, Wonderful': The Time Queen Elizabeth II Watched Maryland Upset UNC." *Washington Post,* 19 Oct. 2017, washingtonpost.com. Accessed 7 Feb. 2024.

2. Benjamin Lorr. *The Secret Life of Groceries: The Dark Miracle of the American Supermarket.* Avery, 2020. 5.

3. Michael Ruhlman. *Grocery: The Buying and Selling of Food in America.* Abrams, 2017. 51.

4. Greg Daugherty. "The Forgotten Protest Movement of the 1960s." *Money,* 19 Oct. 2016, money.com. Accessed 28 Mar. 2024.

5. Jenny McTaggart. "The Golden Years." *Progressive Grocer,* 2 May 2012, progressivegrocer.com. Accessed 27 Mar. 2024.

CHAPTER 3. SATISFYING THE SHOPPER

1. Pamela N. Danziger. "Smart Carts May Be the Disruptive Technology Grocery Stores Need." *Forbes*, 3 Aug. 2023, forbes.com. Accessed 24 Mar. 2024.

2. Richard W. Stevenson. "No Frills, No Sales." *New York Times,* 5 Oct. 1986, nytimes.com. Accessed 2 Apr. 2024.

3. "About Us." *Costco Wholesale*, n.d., costco.com. Accessed 30 Mar. 2024.

4. "ALDI History." *ALDI*, n.d., corporate.aldi.us. Accessed 30 Mar. 2024.

5. Katie Jackson. "What Is Lidl? Why This Discount Grocery Store Is Giving Aldi a Run for Its Money." *Today*, 18 June 2020, today.com. Accessed 30 Mar. 2024.

6. "Growth in the Number of US Farmers Markets Slows in Recent Years." *US Department of Agriculture*, 10 Aug. 2022, ers.usda.gov. Accessed 2 Apr. 2024.

7. Sam Roberts. "Stew Leonard Sr. Dies at 93; Founded 'Disneyland of Dairy Stores.'" *New York Times,* 27 Apr. 2023, nytimes.com. Accessed 1 Apr. 2024.

8. Roberts, "Stew Leonard Sr. Dies at 93."

CHAPTER 4. FROM FARM TO SHELF

1. Paco Underhill. *How We Eat: The Brave New World of Food and Drink.* Simon & Schuster, 2022. 88.

2. Michael Ruhlman. *Grocery: The Buying and Selling of Food in America.* Abrams, 2017. 205.

3. Ruhlman, *Grocery*, 74.

4. Ruhlman, *Grocery*, 69.

5. Benjamin Lorr. *The Secret Life of Groceries: The Dark Miracle of the American Supermarket.* Avery, 2020. 133.

6. Louis Biscotti. "From Buy Buy Brands to Bye Bye Brands? How Private Label Is Beginning to Win F&B Brand Wars." *Forbes,* 10 May 2023, forbes.com. Accessed 3 Apr. 2024.

CHAPTER 5. THE PSYCHOLOGY OF SUPERMARKETS

1. Vance Packard. *The Hidden Persuaders*. Rev. ed., Ig, 2007. 113–114.

2. Michael Y. Park. "How to Buy Food: The Psychology of the Supermarket." *Bon Appétit*, 30 Oct. 2014, bonappetit.com. Accessed 8 Feb. 2024.

3. Michael Ruhlman. *Grocery: The Buying and Selling of Food in America.* Abrams, 2017. 70.

4. Benjamin Lorr. *The Secret Life of Groceries: The Dark Miracle of the American Supermarket.* Avery, 2020. 5.

5. Heather Haddon. "Getting Your Product on Shelves at Whole Foods Just Got Harder." *Wall Street Journal*, 8 Feb. 2018, wsj.com. Accessed 7 Feb. 2024.

6. Julia Russo. "The Hidden Battle Over Grocery Store Shelves." *Sporkful*, 15 Jan. 2024, sporkful.com. Accessed 3 Apr. 2024.

7. Rebecca Rupp. "Surviving the Sneaky Psychology of Supermarkets." *National Geographic,* 14 June 2015, nationalgeographic.com. Accessed 8 Feb. 2024.

CHAPTER 6. ISSUES WITH MODERN SUPERMARKETS

1. Jennifer Earl. "Whole Foods Responds to $6 Pre-Peeled Orange Twitterstorm." *CBS News*, 8 Mar. 2016, cbsnews.com. Accessed 9 Apr. 2024.

2. Earl, "Whole Foods Twitterstorm."

3. Earl, "Whole Foods Twitterstorm."

4. Alejandra Borunda. "Grocery Stores Are Packed with Plastic. Some Are Changing." *National Geographic,* 22 Apr. 2019, nationalgeographic.com. Accessed 8 Feb. 2024.

5. "Report Reveals that U.S. Plastics Recycling Rate Has Fallen to <6%." *Beyond Plastics*, 2021, beyondplastics.org. Accessed 22 July 2023.

6. Jeff Wells and Sam Silverstein. "John Mackey and Whole Foods: A Timeline." *Grocery Dive,* 1 Oct. 2021, grocerydive.com. Accessed 13 Apr. 2024.

7. Borunda, "Grocery Stores Are Packed with Plastic."

8. Bee Wilson. "How Ultra-Processed Food Took Over Your Shopping Basket." *Guardian,* 12 Feb. 2020, theguardian.com. Accessed 7 Apr. 2024.

9. Joe Pinsker. "Grocery Stores: An American Miracle." *Atlantic,* 25 May 2017, theatlantic.com. Accessed 7 Feb. 2024.

10. Jon Keegan. "Forget Milk and Eggs: Supermarkets Are Having a Fire Sale on Data about You." *Markup*, 16 Feb. 2023, themarkup.org. Accessed 3 Apr. 2024.

11. Lauren Hirsch. "What the $24.6 Billion Kroger-Albertsons Merger Could Mean for Groceries." *New York Times,* 14 Oct. 2022, nytimes.com. Accessed 8 Feb. 2024.

12. Clay Venetis. "How Supermarket Mergers Affect Food Deserts." *Modern Farmer,* 22 Nov. 2023, modernfarmer.com. Accessed 7 Apr. 2024.

13. Venetis, "Supermarket Mergers."

14. James Devitt. "What Really Happens When a Grocery Store Opens in a 'Food Desert'?" *New York University*, 10 Dec. 2019, nyu.edu. Accessed 7 Apr. 2024.

CHAPTER 7. COVID-19 AND ONLINE SHOPPING

1. Tara Parker-Pope. "Who Knew Grocery Shopping Could Be So Stressful?" *New York Times,* 26 Mar. 2020, nytimes.com. Accessed 11 Apr. 2024.

2. "America's Largest Food & Retail Union Confirms Growing COVID-19 Impact on Frontline Workers." *United Food and Commercial Workers*, 7 Sep. 2020, ufcw.org. Accessed 12 Apr. 2024.

3. Ian Bogost. "The Supermarket after the Pandemic." *Atlantic,* 17 Apr. 2020, theatlantic.com. Accessed 7 Feb. 2024.

4. Bogost, "Supermarket after the Pandemic."

5. Warren Shoulberg. "The Grocery Business Is Anything But, in the Bag." *Robin Report*, 14 July 2021, therobinreport.com. Accessed 4 Apr. 2024.

6. "The PG 100: The Biggest Players in Grocery Retail." *Progressive Grocer*, 17 May 2023, progressivegrocer.com. Accessed 29 Mar. 2024.

7. "Online Grocery Shopping Statistics." *Capital One Shopping*, 6 Jan. 2024, capitaloneshopping.com. Accessed 26 Mar. 2024.

8. Melinda Sheckells. "Inside Meow Wolf's New Omega Mart Interactive Experience in Las Vegas." *Hollywood Reporter,* 16 Feb. 2021, hollywoodreporter.com. Accessed 1 Apr. 2024.

CHAPTER 8. SUPERMARKETS OF TOMORROW

1. Danny Edsall, et al. "Gen AI Goes Grocery Shopping." *Deloitte Consumer Industry Center*, n.d., deloitte.com. Accessed 23 Mar. 2024.

2. Kaitlyn Tiffany. "Wouldn't It Be Better If Self-Checkout Just Died?" *Vox*, 2 Oct. 2018, vox.com. Accessed 8 Feb. 2024.

3. "Amazon Ditches Cashierless Checkout System at Its Grocery Stores." *CNBC*, 3 Apr. 2024, cnbc.com. Accessed 12 Apr. 2024.

4. "Stop & Shop Upgrades Marty the Robot at 300-Plus Locations." *Supermarket News*, 18 Sept. 2023, supermarketnews.com. Accessed 22 Mar. 2024.

5. "Kroger Fulfillment Network Expands with Customer Fulfillment Center in Denver Metro Area." *Kroger*, 21 June 2022, ir.kroger.com. Accessed 22 Mar. 2024.

6. Melissa Repko. "Here's How Kroger Is Using Robots to Get Groceries to Customers' Doors." *CNBC*, 4 Nov. 2021, cnbc.com. Accessed 22 Mar. 2024.

7. Bill Wilson. "Kroger Reportedly Slows Ocado Fulfillment Center Rollout." *Supermarket News,* 30 May 2023, supermarketnews.com. Accessed 22 Mar. 2024.

8. Repko, "Kroger Is Using Robots."

9. Mark Hamstra. "Supermarkets and Startups Offer Big Lessons on Driverless Product Delivery." *US Chamber of Commerce*, 29 Nov. 2022, uschamber.com. Accessed 23 Mar. 2024.

10. Ali Francis. "Will I See Lab-Grown Meat in Supermarkets Any Time Soon?" *Bon Appétit,* 20 Jan. 2023, bonappetit.com. Accessed 26 Mar. 2024.

11. "What Is Vertical Farming? Everything You Should Know about This Innovation." *Eden Green Technology*, 9 Jan. 2023, edengreen.com. Accessed 14 Apr. 2024.

12. Danny Edsall. "The Future of Grocery Retail." *Deloitte Consumer Industry Center*, 22 Aug. 2023, deloitte.com. Accessed 4 June 2024.

LIZ SONNEBORN

A graduate of Swarthmore College, Liz Sonneborn has written more than 100 books for young readers and adults on a wide variety of subjects. Her specialties include American history, world history, biography, women's studies, and African-American studies. Sonneborn is a longtime resident of Brooklyn, New York.